RED-LETTER PRESS, INC.
Saddle River, NJ 07458

DEDICATED
TO YOU,
THE DOG LOVER

RED-LETTER PRESS, INC.
P.O. Box 393
Saddle River, NJ 07458
www.Red-LetterPress.com
info@Red-LetterPress.com

celebrating DOGS

Compiled by: Jack Kreismer

Creative: Russ Edwards

Editorial: Ellen Fischbein

Cover & Design: Cliff Behum

Contributors:

Jeff Kreismer

Kobus Reyneke

Lori Walsh

celebrating
DOGS

Relishing
the Relationship

True Tales of Heroic Hounds

43-year-old Allen Parton was struck by a car and thrown from his wheelchair. Fortunately, a fast-thinking rescuer immediately moved Mr. Parton into a safe place, covered him with a blanket and brought him a phone. The rescuer also signaled for help and remained at the injured man's side at the scene, in the ambulance and even at the hospital during treatment.

The hero's name was Endal, a five-year-old yellow Labrador Retriever.

"Riva" and "Salty" were two guide dogs that saved their owner's lives just before the World Trade Center in New York collapsed. Riva and Salty guided their blind owners, Mr. Roselle and Mr. Hingson, down the crowded, smoke-filled stairs from the 71st floor and were later honored for their bravery.

An apple a day might keep the doctor away but thank goodness for Debbie Parkhurst that it didn't keep her two-year-old Golden Retriever away. The dog, which goes by the name of Toby, sensed something was wrong when Debbie started choking on an apple. After her own attempts to dislodge it failed, Toby snapped into

celebrating **DOGS**

action, knocking her down and jumping up and down on her chest until the piece of apple was dislodged. He then started licking her to keep her from passing out. Toby's quick actions are credited with saving Ms. Parkhurst's life.

Belle the Beagle bit her owner's cell phone and managed to dial emergency services. When the paramedics arrived at the Florida home, they found that Belle's owner was suffering from a severe diabetic seizure. Belle had been trained to sniff her owner's breath and detect the condition but dialing 911 was a neat "feet".

A Pennsylvania toddler had wandered away from home wearing nothing but a T-shirt in 32-degree weather. The baby was also near a 30-foot precipice, which overhung a busy street. When RC, a German shepherd-husky mix spotted the child, he nudged him back to his outdoor bed of straw and sat on the child to keep him warm. They were both found safe and snug about 9 o'clock the next morning.

Trivia Treats

In 1972, in South Wales, a male dachshund was said to have snuck up on a sleeping female Great Dane. The result: 13 "Great Dachsunds," with short legs, large heads, and raised ears.

celebrating DOGS

FEELIN' GOOD

There's just something about dogs that makes you feel good. You come home; they're thrilled to see you. They're good for the ego.
–*Janet Schulman*

With the exception of women, there is nothing on earth so agreeable or necessary to the comfort of man as the dog.
–*Edward Jesse*

One reason a dog can be such a comfort when you're feeling blue is that he doesn't try to find out why. –*Unknown*

The psychological and moral comfort of a presence at once humble and understanding - this is the greatest benefit that the dog has bestowed upon man. –*Percy Bysshe Shelley*

I like any dog that makes me look good when it stands next to me. –*Jean Harlow*

celebrating DOGS

Norman was walking his dog when the seductive smell of an Italian restaurant called him to lunch. He decided to take his Chihuahua into the restaurant with him, so he donned dark glasses and tapped his way into the establishment.

The waiter said, "Hey Mister- you can't bring a dog in here."

Norman indignantly replied, "I'm blind and this is my Seeing Eye dog."

"You trying to tell me this Chihuahua is a Seeing Eye dog?" the waiter demanded.

"What?" cried Norman, "they gave me a Chihuahua?"

A dog owner takes his ailing pet to the vet. The vet examines the dog and diagnoses it terminally ill. The dog's owner asks for a second opinion. With that, the vet brings his own kitten into the examining room. The kitten examines the sick dog and shakes his head sadly. The sick dog's owner then asks for one more opinion so the vet brings in his Labrador retriever. The Retriever sniffs the dog all over, licks it in various areas and then shakes his head as well. The pet owner is now sadly convinced of his dog's fate. He asks the vet how much he owes for the exam. The vet says $550. When the dog's owner squalks at the bill and asks how come it's so much, the vet replies, "The exam was only $50. It was an additional $500 for the cat scan and lab test."

A fellow with a dog act goes to Hollywood for an interview with a talent agent. He brings his little Shitzu and St. Bernard into the agent's office. Right away, the Shitzu walks to the middle of the office floor and announces to the agent that he'd like to tell a few jokes. Following one hilarious joke after another, the agent says, "Wow, that Shitzu's unbelievable!"

The dog owner says, "The Shitzu's nothing. The St. Bernard is a ventriloquist!"

Two dogs happen to pass by a parking meter. One says to the other, "How do you like that? Pay toilets."

Then there was the guy who named his dog Herpes 'cause he wouldn't heel!

A classified ad appears in the newspaper for a computer-literate, speed typist who can take dictation and speak more than one language.

celebrating **DOGS**

A dog shows up for an interview. It can type better than a hundred words per minute, its dictation capabilities are superior and has computer skills second to none. The prospective boss notices all these wonderful things the dog can do and says to the pooch, "You seem perfect for the job, but you know, it requires you to be able to speak another language. What do you have to say about that?"

The dog looks at the would-be employer and says, "Meow!"

What do you call a dog that hears voices?
A Shih-Tzu-Phrenic

A pooch pays for a help wanted ad allowing for ten words. On the form, the dog fills out, "Woof, woof, woof, woof, woof, woof, woof, woof, woof."

The clerk takes a look at the ad and says, "You've only filled in nine words here. You're entitled to another woof for the same price."

The dog answers, "But that would be silly."

celebrating **DOGS**

A LIFETIME OF LOYALTY

Each year on April 8th at Shibuya railroad station in Japan, hundreds of dog lovers pay homage to the loyalty of an Akita dog, Hachiko, the faithful pet of Dr. Eisaburo Ueno, a professor at Tokyo University. Hachiko, born in 1923, would meet his master at the train station every evening when he returned from work until the night of May 21, 1925, when the professor suffered a stroke and died at the university. The next day and for the next nine years, Hachiko returned to the station and waited for his beloved master before walking home, alone. Hachiko continued to do so until his own death in March, 1934.

celebrating DOGS

DEDICATED DOG

In 2003, 55-year-old Bruce Ashworth, who suffers from multiple sclerosis and uses a wheelchair, slipped and fell into his bathtub. Unable to reach the safety handles on the tub, he couldn't lift himself out. Ashworth's service dog, Libby, retrieved a phone and brought it to him, but the battery was not charged. Ashworth would be stuck for a total of six days, during which time he drifted in and out of consciousness. Ashworth later explained he thought he was going to die and credited Libby with keeping him alive.

As the days stretched on, the trained dog would lick his face to get his attention and slap her paws on the floor to wake him up. A van driver for the disabled who had come to pick him up for a scheduled trip finally rescued Ashworth. When no one answered, the driver found her own way to enter the house- through a dog door specially made for Libby to enter and exit the home.

celebrating DOGS

Man's Best Friend

No man can be condemned for owning a dog. As long as he has a dog, he has a friend; and the poorer he gets, the better friend he has. *–Will Rogers*

Dogs are such agreeable friends-they ask no questions, they pass no criticisms. *– George Eliot*

My dogs forgive anger in me, the arrogance in me, the brute in me. They forgive everything I do before I forgive myself. *–Guy de la Valdene*

The greatest pleasure of a dog is that you may make a fool of yourself with him, and not only will he not scold you, but he will make a fool of himself, too. *–Samuel Butler*

Thorns may hurt you, men desert you, sunlight turn to fog; but you're never friendless ever, if you have a dog. *–Douglas Mallock*

He is your friend, your partner, your defender, your dog. You are

celebrating **DOGS**

his life, his love, his leader. He will be yours, faithful and true, to the last beat of his heart. You owe it to him to be worthy of such devotion. *–Unknown*

One of the most enduring friendships in history - dogs and their people, people and their dogs. *–Terry Kay*

Blessed is the person who has earned the love of an old dog. *–Sidney Jeanne Seward*

Stick around any place long enough and chances are you'll be taken for granted. Hang around for 20,000 years wagging your tail and being man's (and woman's) best friend, and you'll be taken for granted big time. *–Lynn Van Matre*

When a man's best friend is his dog, that dog has a problem. *–Edward Abbey*

The dog has been esteemed and loved by all the people on earth and he has deserved this affection for he renders services that have made him man's best friend. *–Alfred Barbou*

celebrating DOGS

My dear old dog, most constant of all friends.
–*William Croswell Doane*

Outside of a dog, a book is a man's best friend, and inside a dog, it's too dark to read. – *Groucho Marx*

Properly trained, a man can be dog's best friend. – *Corey Ford*

Histories are more full of examples of the fidelity of dogs than of friends. –*Alexander Pope*

Everyone needs a spiritual guide: a minister, rabbi, counselor, wise friend, or therapist. My own wise friend is my dog.
–*Gary Kowalski*

Pet a dog where he can't scratch and he'll always be your friend. –*Orville Mars*

Isn't it wonderful how dogs can win friends and influence people without ever reading a book? – *E.C. McKenzie*

celebrating DOGS

If you want to be liked, get a dog. The people you work with are not your friends. *–Deborah Norville*

They say a dog is man's best friend, but I don't buy it. How many of your friends have had you neutered? *–Larry Reeb*

Trivia Treats

Not Feeling Up To Par: In April of 2004, an eighteen-month-old German shepherd named Libby underwent a two and a half hour operation after coughing up blood. When vets operated on her, they discovered that she had swallowed twenty-eight golf balls.

In 1937, Helen Keller became the first recipient of an Akita in America, a puppy which a Japanese policeman brought to her as a gift.

Pluto, best known as the dog of Mickey Mouse, did not take up his famous role until his third cartoon. He first appeared in *The Chain Gang* in 1930 and then *The Mouse Hunt* in '31.

Poppy ♥ Love

Whoever said you can't buy happiness forgot little puppies.
–*Gene Hill*

Buy a pup and your money will buy love unflinching.
–*Rudyard Kipling*

A puppy plays with every pup he meets, but an old dog has few associates. –*Josh Billings*

If a picture wasn't going very well, I'd put a puppy dog into it.
–*Norman Rockwell*

Of all the things I miss from veterinary practice, puppy breath is one of the fondest memories! –*Dr. Tom Cat*

Puppies are nature's remedy for feeling unloved, plus numerous other ailments of life. –*Richard Allan Palm*

There is no psychiatrist in the world like a puppy licking your face.
–*Bern Williams*

When you feel lousy, puppy therapy is indicated. –*Sara Paretsky*

celebrating DOGS

No symphony orchestra ever played music like a two-year-old girl laughing with a puppy.   *–Bern Williams*

Inside every Newfoundland, Boxer, Elkhound and Great Dane is a puppy longing to climb on to your lap. *–Helen Thomson*

Trivia Treats

About those dog years: That formula- 7 of our years to 1 dog year –isn't really up to snuff. "They" say the first year of a puppy's life is actually about 21 human years. Every year after that is equal to approximately 4 human years. Then again, "they" say toy-dog breeds live an average seven years longer than large breeds. Then again…

Hilary Swank, who went through five months of training and sparring in preparation for her role in *Million Dollar Baby*, arrived on the set one day with her first serious injury- a black eye courtesy of Karoo, her 20-pound Corgi/Jack Russell. Besides the obvious shiner, she was nursing a bruised ego having been KOed by K-9.

A bloodhound is the only dog whose evidence is admissible in court.

celebrating DOGS

*I think dogs
are the most amazing
creatures. They give
unconditional love. For me
they are the role models
for being alive.*

–Gilda Radner

MIXED BREEDS

Cross a Pointer with a Setter and you'll get
a Poinsetter- a traditional Christmas pet.

Cross a Malamute with a Pointer and you'll get a
Moot Point- Not that it matters anyway.

Cross an Irish Water Spaniel with an English Springer Spaniel and
you'll get an Irish Springer- a dog fresh and clean as a whistle.

Cross a Pekingese with a Lhasa Apso and you'll get a
Peekasso- an abstract dog.

Cross a Terrier with a Bulldog and you'll get a
Terribull- a dog prone to awful mistakes.

Cross a Great Pyrenees with a Dachshund and you'll get
Pyradachs- a puzzling breed.

Cross a Newfoundland with a Basset Hound and you'll get a
Newfound Asset Hound- a dog for financial advisors.

celebrating DOGS

PUP-POURRI

Dalmatian puppies are born completely white.

More than 5 million puppies are born every year in America.

A puppy's temperament and personality are shaped by the experiences the dog shares with littermates.

During the first few weeks of their lives, puppies often twitch while they sleep, as if they are dreaming. The twitching is actually part of activated sleep, which is meant to strengthen the puppies' muscles so they will be strong enough to stand up and walk.

A puppy is capable of learning, and making conscious decisions, at only three weeks old.

By the time a puppy is eight to ten weeks old, its brain is fully functional.

Puppies sleep ninety percent of the day for their first few weeks.

Puppies can hiccup.

celebrating DOGS

DANIEL AND THE DACHSHUND

On a rainy September day in Norway in 2003, one diminutive Dachshund came up a huge hero. Ivar Lunde and his dog, Agathon, had driven down to a rocky beach for Agathon's regular walk. However, with high winds and stormy weather, Lunde decided it would be best to stay in his car and let the eight-year-old dog walk himself. After a while, Lunde called for the small pup, but Agathon simply sat still, barking. Finally, the dog ran back to the car, but refused to get in.

Lunde said Agathon, constantly looking back to make sure his master was following, led him to a waterfront. Just off the shore, a soaked child was found clinging to a slippery rock. Daniel, a four-year-old boy, had wandered away from his mother at a store checkout counter, and had been reported missing for several hours. Lunde managed to carry a soaked Daniel safely to shore and immediately contacted the police. Unharmed, Daniel would be reunited with his mother, and Agathon would later be rewarded as a national hero of Norway.

celebrating DOGS

THE FRIENDSHIP OF A DOG IS
PRECIOUS. IT BECOMES EVEN
MORE SO WHEN ONE IS SO FAR
REMOVED FROM HOME....I HAVE
A SCOTTIE. IN HIM I FIND
CONSOLATION AND DIVERSION....
HE IS THE ONE PERSON TO
WHOM I CAN TALK WITHOUT
THE CONVERSATION COMING
BACK TO WAR.

- DWIGHT D. EISENHOWER

celebrating **DOGS**

PRESIDENTIAL
POOCHES

When Oval Office meetings dragged on too long, President Gerald Ford whistled for his Golden Retriever, Liberty. The feisty dog would rush in and pounce on people, which quickly broke up the meeting… Liberty gave birth to nine puppies in the White House.

Teddy Roosevelt's pit bull, Pete, once tore off the French ambassador's pants at the White House. He must have had his heart broken once by a poodle.

President Lyndon Johnson had two beagles named Him and Her. He caused a national uproar when he picked his dogs up by the ears.

President Franklin Delano Roosevelt took his Scotch terrier, Fala, everywhere with him. In fact, Fala was nicknamed "The Informer" by the Secret Service men guarding FDR. The president's travel plans were kept secret during World War II but Fala insisted going for a walk at every train stop, thus tipping off that FDR couldn't be far away.

FDR once deployed a destroyer to the Aleutian Islands to retrieve his Scottie, who had been accidentally left behind.

Over FDR's 12 years and one month as president, 11 dogs lived in the White House: a Bullmastiff, two Red Setters, a Retriever, a Bulldog, a Llewellin Setter, a Scotch Terrier, a Great Dane, a Sheepdog and a German Shepherd.

George Washington kept 36 foxhounds. One was named Sweetlips. Wonder how he knew?

Ulysses S. Grant's dog was a Newfoundland named "Faithful".

Barbara Bush's book about her English Springer Spaniel, Millie, was on the bestseller list for 29 weeks. Published in 1991, the book earned almost $900,000 in royalties. "First Dog" Millie earned well more than four times the salary that George W. Bush made as president that year.

The biggest and the smallest dogs to live in the White House were both there during the administration of President James Buchanan. The president had a Newfoundland named Lara. As the president wasn't married, his niece Harriet Lane lived there as White House hostess with her tiny toy terrier named Punch.

John F. Kennedy's terrier, Charlie, sired 4 puppies with Russian space dog Laika's daughter, Pushinka. At least Cold War politics didn't come between puppy love.

celebrating DOGS

JFK requested that his dogs meet the presidential helicopter when the president arrived at the White House.

Warren Harding owned an Airedale called Laddie Boy and a Bulldog called Oh Boy. Laddie Boy had his own chair so he could sit in at cabinet meetings.

Ronald Reagan owned two dogs as president, a Cavalier King Charles Spaniel called Rex and a Bouvier des Flandres named Lucky. The president was once photographed being dragged across the White House lawn by Lucky in the presence of Margaret Thatcher. It was quite a breach of etiquette; Margaret wanted to drag him herself.

Bill Clinton's Chocolate Labrador Retriever, Buddy, reportedly didn't get along with the first family cat, "Socks". Buddy suspected Socks was keeping an eye on Bill and reporting back to Hillary.

Checkers was Richard Nixon's dog while he was vice president, but when he was at the White House, presidential pooches included "Vicky" the Poodle, "Pasha" the Terrier and "King Timahoe", an Irish Setter.

Abraham Lincoln's dog was named Jip.

celebrating DOGS

THE HEALTH OF IT

Asthma doesn't seem to bother me any more unless I'm around cigars or dogs. The thing that would bother me most would be a dog smoking a cigar. *–Steve Allen*

Dogs manufacture their own vitamin C.

While it is not believed that dogs can get Alzheimer's disease, older dogs may show signs of confusion and forgetfulness. Veterinarians refer to this as "canine cognitive dysfunction" and can provide medication for treatment.

A dog's temperature is between 100.2-102.8 degrees Fahrenheit.

As a dog grows, its mental sharpness decreases. A young dog's nervous system transmits messages at a rate of about 20,000 feet per second. Later in life, this falls to nearly 4,000 feet per second

Obesity is the #1 health problem among dogs.

celebrating DOGS

A study of recovery rates in heart failure patients found that a twelve minute visit by a dog reduced levels of stress hormone by 17%...That's 15% higher than when humans visited alone.

Some dogs can predict when a child will have an epileptic seizure, and even protect the child from injury. They're not trained to do this, but simply learn to respond after observing at least one attack.

Researchers have discovered that dogs often have the ability to smell the presence of autism in children.

GRRROANERS

Patient: Doc, I feel like a dog.
Doctor: How long have you felt this way?
Patient: Ever since I was a puppy.

How do you make a dog disappear?
Use Spot remover.

Two fleas were outside the Empire State Building, heading up to New York's Central Park when one says to the other, "Shall we walk or take a dog?"

What do you do with a broken dog?
Get him fixed.

In the old West one day, a Basset Hound hobbles into town with a heavily bandaged foot. The Dodge City sheriff says, "What's up, podna'?" The Basset answers, "I'm lookin' for the dog who shot my paw."

It was so hot, a dog was seen chasing a cat and they were both walking.

Q: How do you telephone a police dog?
A: Dial K911.

Then there was a dog that saw a sign, WET PAINT. He did.

Did you hear about the Pekingese dog that married a tomcat?
Now they have a Peking Tom.

celebrating **DOGS**

A Decorated Dog

Sergeant Stubby, described as an "American Bull Terrier" and recognized as America's first ever trained war dog, served eighteen months on the front during World War I. Stubby was under constant fire, and even though he was wounded in the foreleg by a hand grenade, he would return to the trenches. After being gassed himself, Stubby was able to save his regiment from surprise poison gas attacks. Since he could hear the whine of incoming artillery shells before humans, Stubby was also able to tell his unit when to duck for cover. The prized pooch was even solely responsible for capturing a German spy.

Sergeant Stubby was recognized for his contributions by trips to the White House and became the only dog to be promoted to sergeant through combat, personally decorated by General John Pershing. He was also made a lifetime member of the American Legion, the Red Cross, and the YMCA. Perhaps most importantly, Stubby's efforts inspired the creation of the U.S. "K-9 Corps", in preparation for World War II. There, dogs were trained and prepared for battlefield action, in hopes of creating another wartime hero.

celebrating DOGS

Top Ten Most Popular Dog Names in the United States

Male	Female
Max	Maggie
Jake	Molly
Buddy	Lady
Bailey	Sadie
Sam	Lucy
Rocky	Daisy
Buster	Ginger
Casey	Abby
Cody	Sasha
Duke	Sandy

celebrating DOGS

Aesop's Fable

In the sixth century B.C., Aesop, a freed slave, compiled collections of brief fables. These famous stories, which teach basic life lessons, often involve personified animals such as dogs. Here is one dog owners should keep in mind:

The Old Hound

An old hound, which in the days of his youth and strength had never yielded to any beast of the forest, encountered in his old age a boar in the chase. He seized him boldly by the ear, but could not retain his hold because of the decay of his teeth, so that the boar escaped. His master, quickly coming up, was very much disappointed, and fiercely abused the dog. The hound looked up and said, "It was not my fault, Master; my spirit was as good as ever, but I could not help my infirmities. I rather deserve to be praised for what I have been, than to be blamed for what I am."

Dollars To Dogs

In 1932, in the depths of the Great Depression, the American million-airess, Ella Wendal, left a legacy of 75 million dollars in her will to her standard poodle called "Toby". That kind of gives the term "Doggie - Diamonds" a whole new meaning.

27% of Americans mention their dog in their will and an estimated 1,000,000 dogs in the U.S. have been named as the primary beneficiaries in their owner's will.

According to a Gallup poll, 63% of dogs get Christmas presents from their owners, 58% of cats.

Two 1903 paintings recently sold at auction for $590,000 - the paintings were in the famous Dogs Playing Poker series.

Dog owners spend an average of 6 percent of their grocery bill on their pet. Together, dogs and cats consume almost $7 billion worth of pet food a year.

USA Today reported that 38% of dog owners said they would spend "any amount" to save their pet's life.

celebrating DOGS

MAN IS DOG'S BEST FRIEND TOO

During the 2003 Fourth of July weekend in West Virginia, an injured black Labrador limped up to the Beckley Appalachian Regional Hospital. The dog, apparently hit by a car, entered the building by triggering the automatic sensors which opened the sliding glass doors. He then waited for assistance in the hallway. Hospital workers, stunned at the sight, gave the dog water and called in a veterinarian, offering to pay the unknown animal's bill.

After no one claimed the dog, BAHR housekeeping staff member Nancy Massey took him home with her. However, while being kept outside in the yard, the rescued dog slipped out of his collar and ran away. Massey searched through the night for him, but to no avail.

The very next day, a woman named Betty Ellison called her veterinarian's office to say that her dog Jasper, who disappeared on July 4th, had returned home. Indeed, the 13-year-old Lab mix was identified as the same dog that had been hit by the car. After finding his way to the hospital, Jasper had found his way back home - nearly 15 miles from Massey's backyard.

celebrating DOGS

FAITHFUL TILL THE END

In 2003, residents of Togliatti, Russia, raised $8,000 to erect a bronze statue of a local icon, a dog named Faithful. Until the day he died, the German shepherd refused to leave the spot where his owners were killed in a car accident. Faithful survived on the food and water that people began bringing him after he refused their attempts to find him a new home. He would spend a total of seven years watching over his loved ones, until finally joining them.

celebrating DOGS

You think dogs
will not be in Heaven?
I tell you, they will be there
long before any of us.

-Robert Louis Stevenson

Screen Test

Not all have left their paw prints (nor anything else) on Hollywood's Walk of Fame but they all left an impression on moviegoers. See if you can fetch the answers to these trivia questions:

1. What was the name of Jerry Reed's Basset Hound in *Smokey and the Bandit?*

2. Going way back, what four-footed ham was *The Thin Man's* best friend?

3. In *National Lampoon's Christmas Vacation* what was the name of Cousin Eddie's pooch?

4. What breed of dog starred in the *Beethoven* series?

5. Higgins, who played the title character of 1974's fifth highest grossing film, previously appeared in a long-running TV show. For the Trivia Blue Ribbon, name the movie and TV show.

ANSWERS:

1. Fred 2. Asta 3. Snot 4. Saint Bernard 5. Benji and Petticoat Junction

celebrating **DOGS**

DOG OF WAR

Jack, a Bull Terrier, was a popular and reliable member of the volunteer firemen of Niagara, Pennsylvania, as he searched out dead and wounded soldiers after battles during the Civil War. Jack escaped capture by Confederate soldiers and survived the battle of Antietam in 1862, which killed and wounded 23,000 soldiers. When Jack was eventually captured by the Confederates, he was exchanged, according to wartime protocol, for a Confederate prisoner and returned to his regiment.

celebrating DOGS

A Small Price To Pay

Dogs have given us their absolute all. We are the center of their universe. We are the focus of their love and faith and trust. They serve us in return for scraps. It is without a doubt the best deal man has ever made. –*Roger Caras*

They give unconditional love and undying loyalty in return for regular meals and an occasional pat on the head. –*Jon Winokur*

I guess you don't really own a dog, you rent them, and you have to be thankful that you had a long lease. –*Joe Garagiola*

There's a saying. If you want someone to love you forever, buy a dog, feed it and keep it around. –*Dick Dale*

He never makes it his business to inquire whether you are in the right or wrong, never bothers as to whether you are going up or down life's ladder, never asks whether you are rich or poor, silly or wise, sinner or saint. You are his pal. That is enough for him. –*Jerome K. Jerome*

If you would invest in friendship, buy a dog. –*Le Baron Cooke*

A Shaggy Dog Story

You know it. You've heard it. You may have told it- That extremely long-winded yarn with the pointless punch line. It's been around since way back when. When is that, you ask? Well, no one knows for sure but our dogged research has dug up what we believe to be the original shaggy dog joke. Here goes...

A wealthy English gentleman had his butler place full-page ads in newspapers all over the world, hoping to find his long lost, shaggy sheepdog. The finder's reward was a guarantee of a lifetime of luxury according to the dog-owner's plea. One morning over breakfast, a New York City fellow was reading the *Times* when he came across the advertisement. He didn't think much of it but later that day while strolling through Central Park, the fellow saw a stray sheepdog and recalled that it seemed to fit the description in the newspaper ad. The man left the park to buy a leash, returned and rounded up the pooch. The fellow bought a plane ticket for himself and the dog. They flew to London's Heathrow Airport and then hired a limo to escort them to the address cited in the advertisement. Once they arrived, the fellow rang the doorbell and the butler answered. He looked down at the dog and then said to the fellow, "Ah, yes. We're looking for a shaggy dog, but not so shaggy as that, Sir!"

He is so shaggy. People are amazed when he gets up and they suddenly realize they have been talking to the wrong end. –*Elizabeth Jones*

Trivia Treats

At the tail end of The Beatles' song *A Day in the Life*, an ultrasonic whistle, audible only to dogs, was recorded by Paul McCartney for his Shetland sheepdog.

celebrating DOGS

THE WORLD'S WORST WATCHDOGS

Labradors [are] lousy watchdogs. They usually bark when there is a stranger about, but it is an expression of unmitigated joy at the chance to meet somebody new, not a warning. *–Norman Strung*

When it comes to watchdogs, smaller is usually better. According to Petrix.com, which ranks the best and worst watchdogs, the belief that a large dog is best to protect the home is a common misconception. In alphabetical order, here are ten of the most laid back dog breeds. As you can see, the larger is often the lazier.

---

1. Basset hound
2. Blood hound
3. Bulldog
4. Clumber spaniel
5. Irish wolfhound
6. Newfoundland
7. Old English sheepdog
8. Pug
9. Saint Bernard
10. Scottish deerhound

FELIX AND FIDO

Cats are smarter than dogs. You can't get eight cats to pull a sled through snow. *–Jeff Valdez*

I put contact lenses in my dog's eyes. They had little pictures of cats on them. Then I took one out and he ran around in circles. *–Steven Wright*

You call to a dog and a dog will break its neck to get to you. Dogs just want to please. Call to a cat and its attitude is, "What's in it for me?" *–Lewis Grizzard*

If you can look at a dog and not feel vicarious excitement and affection, you must be a cat. *–Unknown*

Dogs have owners; cats have staff. *–Sanford Mims*

To keep a true perspective of your importance, you should have a dog that will worship you and a cat that will ignore you. *–Rita Kubran*

If a dog jumps in your lap, it is because he is fond of you; but if a cat does the same thing, it is because your lap is warmer. *–Alfred North Whitehead*

Women and cats will do as they please, and men and dogs should relax and get used to the idea. *–Robert A. Heinlein*

celebrating DOGS

"Some of my best leading men have been dogs and horses."
-*Elizabeth Taylor*

Rin Tin Tin signed his own movie contracts with a paw print.

The dog that starred in Disney's *Old Yeller* was named "Spike". He was owned and trained by the Weatherwax family, most famous for training the various Lassies.

The name of that happy dog on the Cracker Jack box is Bingo.

Andy, Marbles, Rover, Olaf, and Spike were his brothers, Belle and Molly his sisters. The dog: Snoopy.

Paul McCartney's Old English sheepdog, Martha, was immortalized in the Beatles' song, *Martha, My Dear*.

The Wizard of Oz's Toto was played by a female Cairn Terrier named Terry.

celebrating DOGS

Doggie Do's and Don'ts

Dogs don't have a sense of "time".

Dogs do have the capability to follow the pointing of a human finger to locate a target, something that neither chimpanzees nor wolves can do.

Dogs don't only use their nose for sensing odors and scents, but also to keep cool. The longer the dog's nose, the better his cooling system works.

Dogs do have great smellers. They have about 220 million scent-detector cells in their nose, compared to a human's 5 million.

Dogs don't yawn because they're tired, but because they're confused.

Dogs do cry. In fact, they have twice as many tear glands as humans.

Dogs do pick up local accents from their owners. For example, a study of British dogs showed that the barks of several pooches showed a variation in pitch and tone corresponding to their owners' voices.

celebrating DOGS

Man vs. Dog

Dogs love us, but they are very observant animals. I'm sure they notice that we keep the best food for ourselves. –Markoff Chane

If you pick up a starving dog and make him prosperous, he will not bite you. This is the principal difference between a dog and a man. –Mark Twain

Man himself cannot express love and humility by external signs, so plainly as does a dog, when with drooping ears, hanging lips, flexuous body, and wagging tail, he meets his beloved master. – Charles Darwin

Dogs are us, only innocent. –Cynthia Heimel

The more I see of men, the more I admire dogs. –Jeanne-Marie Roland

A dog is not "almost human" and I know of no greater insult to the canine race than to describe it as such. –John Holmes

Don't make the mistake of treating your dogs like humans, or they'll treat you like dogs. –Martha Scott

Wordplay

Jaguars suffer from cynophobia- a fear of dogs.

Fido, as in dog, translates from Latin, as in "I am faithful."

The saying, "Man's best friend" dates back to 1870, when Senator George Graham Vest prosecuted a man for shooting a hound dog. Part of Vest's famous speech that won the case read: "The one absolutely unselfish friend that a man can have in this selfish world, the one that never deserts him... is his dog."

The xoloitzquintli is a Mexican hairless dog.

The Canary Islands were not named for birds. They were named after a breed of large dogs. The Latin name was "Canariae insulae", the "Island of Dogs."

The creation of the term "hot dog" is often attributed to sports cartoonist Thomas A. "Tad" Dorgan. In 1903, Dorgan made a drawing of a sausage in a roll with the sausage resembling a dachshund.

celebrating DOGS

The Bassett Hound name comes from the French word "bas," meaning "low," because the dog's body is so low to the ground.

The "dog days" of summer actually have no canine connection. They are so-named because that period marks the time of year when Sirius (the Dog Star) is seen rising and setting with the sun.

Terrier comes from the Latin word "terra" meaning "earth."

English royalty allowed small dogs to sit on their laps because the fleas favored the dogs over the people, and would jump to the royal pups. Thus, the origin of the phrase "Lap Dogs."

Trivia Treats

A study done at Queen's University in Belfast revealed that dogs are appeased by classical music, indifferent to pop and disturbed by heavy metal music.

When performing his hit song *Hound Dog* on *The Steve Allen Show*, Elvis Presley sang to a Basset Hound named Sherlock.

celebrating DOGS

In a Dog's Eyes

I've seen a look in dogs' eyes, a quickly vanishing look of amazed contempt, and I am convinced that basically dogs think humans are nuts. *–John Steinbeck*

My dog is usually pleased with what I do, because she is not infected with the concept of what I should be doing.
–Lonzo Idolswine

Man is a dog's idea of what God should be. *–Holbrook Jackson*

If a dog's prayers were answered, bones would rain from the sky.
–Old Proverb

If a dog will not come to you after having looked you in the face, you should go home and examine your conscience.
–Woodrow Wilson

I wonder what goes through his mind when he sees us peeing in his water bowl. *–Penny Ward Moser*

Ever consider what they must think of us? I mean, here we come back from a grocery store with the most amazing haul - chicken, pork, half a cow. They must think we're the greatest hunters on earth! *–Anne Tyler*

To his dog, every man is King; hence the constant popularity of dogs. *– Aldous Huxley*

If you are a dog and your owner suggests that you wear a sweater, suggest that he wear a tail. *–Fran Lebowitz*

From the dog's point of view, his master is an elongated and abnormally cunning dog. *–Mabel Louise Robinson*

To your dog, you are the greatest, the smartest, the nicest human being who was ever born. *–Louis Sabin*

I hope to be the kind of person my dog thinks I am. *–Unknown*

Don't accept your dog's admiration as conclusive evidence that you are wonderful. *–Ann Landers*

Sometimes you panic and find yourself emitting remarks so profoundly inane that you would be embarrassed to say them to your dog. Your dog would look at you and think to itself, "I may lick myself in public, but I'd never say anything as stupid as that." *–Dave Barry*

celebrating DOGS

HE NEEDED A DOG LICENSE
AND A MARRIAGE LICENSE

In 2004, a seventy-five-year old man from Nepal named Phulram Chaudhary tied the knot… with his dog. The wedding, which was attended by Chaudhary's son and other relatives, followed a Tharu community custom that is intended to ensure good luck. The custom simply holds that any old man who re-grows his teeth must take a dog to be his "lawfully wedded wife." The honeymoon would not last long, however, as Chaudhary would die three days later. It's a shame. She had promised she would never stray.

celebrating DOGS

CHILD'S PLAY

The dog was created especially for children. He is the god of froic.–Henry Ward Beecher

Dachshunds are ideal dogs for small children, as they are already stretched and pulled to such a length that the child cannot do much harm one way or the other. *–Robert Benchley*

I can still see my first dog. For six years he met me at the same place after school and convoyed me home — a service he thought up himself. A boy doesn't forget that sort of association. *–E.B. White*

Youngsters of the age of two and three are endowed with extraordinary strength. They can lift a dog twice their own weight and dump him into the bathtub. *–Erma Bombeck*

Give a boy a dog and you've furnished him a playmate. *–Berton Braley*

I was three years old. I was messing with my grandparents' dog in Las Vegas, and he decided to pick me up by my head and run around the backyard with me. *–Brian Austin Green*

celebrating **DOGS**

Dog Talk

There is nothing funny about dogs playing poker. There is nothing remotely cute about animals with gambling problems. If you look closely at those paintings, you can tell that most of those dogs are playing with money they can't afford to lose. And sadder still, it takes seven of their dollars to make one of ours. *–Dennis Miller*

I've been on so many blind dates I should get a free dog.
–Wendy Liebman

We've begun to long for the pitter-patter of little feet, so we bought a dog. Well, it's cheaper, and you get more feet. *–Rita Rudner*

Do you realize they have psychiatrists for dogs now? That in and of itself can screw up a dog. "Hey, pal, am I allowed up on the couch, or am I not allowed up on the couch?' *–Dennis Miller*

I'll never forget my youth. I was teacher's pet. She couldn't afford a dog. *–Rodney Dangerfield*

celebrating **DOGS**

The average dog is a nicer person than the average person.

-Andy Rooney

Fido Factoids

In eight years a male greyhound in London sired 2,414 registered puppies as well as 600 others that weren't on the books.

The majority of dogs are double-coated, and average anywhere from 1,000 to 6,000 hairs per square inch.

Scientists have recently claimed that dogs do in fact laugh. This laughter is expressed through "play panting" among joyful canines.

In 1990 the California legislature overturned a ruling that allowed dogs' teeth to be cleaned only by veterinarians.

Strongheart Dog Food was named after the canine film celebrity, who has a star at 1724 Vine Street on the Hollywood Walk of Fame.

Saint Bernard dogs have never been known to carry kegs of brandy.

celebrating DOGS

According to the American Animal Hospital Association, 70% of people sign their pet's name on greeting cards and 58% include their pets in family and holiday portraits.

Houdini trained his pet dog to escape from a paw-sized set of handcuffs.

Like humans, dogs can be right-handed or left-handed (or should that be south "paw"?).

If a female dog mates with more than one dog during her period of conception, it is possible for different puppies in her litter to have different fathers.

The only state to have developed a distinct breed of dog is Maryland with its Chesapeake Bay retriever.

The real name of Eddie, the scrappy dog on TV's *Frasier*, was Moose (who, at 16, died of old age in 2006).

Over 4,000 different dog stamps have been in circulation since the first one was issued in 1877 in Newfoundland.

celebrating DOGS

Dogs In History

Gidget the Chihuahua was the popular advertising figure and mascot used by Taco Bell.

Nipper is famous for staring curiously into a phonograph. He later became the mascot and logo for RCA.

Mick the Miller, a racing greyhound, was the first greyhound to win the English Derby in successive years and the first greyhound to run a 525 yard course in under 30 seconds.

Snuppy, an Afghan hound, was the first dog produced by cloning.

The first dog to star in American cinema was "Jean" the Vitagraph dog, a Border Collie mix, who made his film debut in 1910.

Judy, a ship's dog that served with the Royal Navy, was the only animal to have been officially registered as a Japanese prisoner of war.

Sam, a blind Chinese Crested hairless, won the World's Ugliest Dog Contest three years running.

celebrating DOGS

A USA Customs Labrador named Snag has made 118 drug seizures worth a canine record $810 million. Now that's a canine worth his weight in cocaine.

Laika, a female Siberian Husky mix, became the first animal to enter orbit when she was launched into space aboard the Sputnik 2 mission.

Balto, a world famous sled dog, was in the lead position on the final leg of the 1925 serum run to Nome (which relayed diphtheria medicine via dog sled across Alaska to combat an epidemic). Balto is memorialized with a statue in New York's Central Park where millions of dogs have since paid their respects — in their own doggie way of course.

Trivia Treats

In all of his works, Shakespeare wrote only one part for a dog. The comedic scene, in *Two Gentlemen of Verona*, involves a servant scolding his dog, Crab, for misbehaving.

celebrating DOGS

By the Numbers

87% of dog owners say that their dog curls up beside them or lies next to their feet while they watch T.V.

Cats, not dogs, are the most common pets in America. They outnumber dogs 66 million to 58 million.

88% of dog owners say their pooch has one or more qualities that they'd like to see in their significant other, according to the American Kennel Club.

According to a *New York Times* 2003 report, the average life span of a dog is 12 years, 5 years longer than in 1930.

People spend four times the amount on dog food than they do on baby food.

The average dog's jaws exert 150 to 200 pounds of bite pressure per square inch. Some dogs bite down with a force of up to 450 pounds.

celebrating DOGS

If never spayed or neutered, a female dog, her mate, and their offspring could produce over 66,000 puppies in 6 years!

94% of pet owners say their pet makes them smile more than once a day.

In 2007, Jay Leno reported on the *Tonight Show* that dogs participate in one third of all weddings in the United States.

Only one out of every 130 dogs who try out for police work make the grade.

Approximately 85% of dogs go to a vet over the course of a year.

Pollsters say that 40% of dog and cat owners carry pictures of the pets in their wallets.

Playing the percentages: 63% of Americans sleep with their pets, 33% have talked with their dog on the phone, and 3% have showered with them.

A dog sleeps about 14 hours a day.

celebrating DOGS

DOGMA

No matter how little money and how few possessions you own, having a dog makes you rich. *–Louis Sabin*

Dogs lead a nice life. You never see a dog with a wristwatch. *–George Carlin*

I think we are drawn to dogs because they are the uninhibited creatures we might be if we weren't certain we knew better. *–George Bird Evans*

The more people I meet the more I like my dog. *–Unknown*

Folks will know how large your soul is by the way you treat a dog! *–Charles F. Doran*

I love dogs. They live in the moment and don't care about anything except affection and food. They're loyal and happy. Humans are just too damn complicated. *–David Duchovny*

Never stand between a dog and the hydrant. *–John Peers*

celebrating DOGS

Happiness to a dog is what lies on the other side of the door.
–*Charleton Ogburn*

God ... sat down for a moment when the dog was finished in order
to watch it... and to know that it was good, that nothing was lack-
ing, that it could not have been made better. –*Rainer Maria Rilke*

We derive immeasurable good, uncounted pleasures, enormous
security, and many critical lessons about life by owning dogs.
–*Roger Caras*

The dog has no ambition, no self-interest, no desire for vengeance,
no fear other than that of displeasing. –*Count of Buffon*

Some days you're the dog; some days you're the hydrant. –*Unknown*

Dogs are our link to paradise. They don't know evil or jealousy or dis-
content. To sit with a dog on a hillside on a glorious afternoon is to
be back in Eden, where doing nothing was not boring — it was
peace. –*Milan Kundera*

If I have any beliefs about immortality, it is that certain dogs I have
known will go to heaven, and very, very few persons. –*James Thurber*

celebrating DOGS

Life is like a dogsled team. If you ain't the lead dog, the scenery never changes. –*Lewis Grizzard*

A dog is for life, and not just for Christmas.
–*National Canine Defense League slogan*

I'd be happy to have my biography be the stories of my dogs. To me, to live without dogs would mean accepting a form of blindness.
–*Thomas McGuane*

You really have to be some kind of a creep for a dog to reject you.
–*Joe Garagiola*

Getting a dog is like getting married. It teaches you to be less self-centered, to accept sudden, surprising outbursts of affection, and not to be upset by a few scratches on your car. –*Will Stanton*

When a man's dog turns against him it is time for a wife to pack her trunk and go home to mama. –*Mark Twain.*

To err is human, to forgive canine. –*Unknown*

celebrating DOGS

Through the Ages

Thomas Jefferson introduced the first dog license in the U.S. in the 1880s.

In the 19th century Dalmatians were used to defend carriages against highwaymen and chased away animals that could scare the horses. Apparently they were good dogs to have if you were in a spot.

People in ancient China stayed warm by carrying toy breeds in their sleeves. Wonder if they ever tried an armpit Bull?

Rock 'n' roll band Three Dog Night was named for the way Australian natives kept warm by sleeping with their pets.

General Custer slept with his dog.

One of the oldest breeds, the dachshund, gets its name from the Germans who used it as a hunting dog. "Dachs" means badger and

celebrating DOGS

"Hund" means dog. They were quick, persistent and low to the ground, a great set of attributes to go into tunnels.

The oldest known breed of dog is the Saluki, a prized hunting dog in ancient Egypt. The name means "Noble One" in Arabic.

Dogs were first domesticated by cavemen.

Even though a Newfoundland saved his life when he slipped and fell from a boat, Napoleon Bonaparte had a lifelong hatred of dogs.

The last surviving member of the famous Bonaparte family, Jerome Napoleon Bonaparte, died in 1945 of injuries sustained from tripping over his dog's leash.

The earliest dog fossil dates back to nearly 10,000 B.C.

Homer immortalized the dog as man's most faithful companion as far back as 850 B.C.

Cerberus was the tri-headed dog that guarded the underworld in

Greek mythology.

The Pekingese were sacred to the emperors of ancient China for more than 2,000 years. They also are one of the oldest breeds of dogs in the world.

The Doberman was originally bred in Germany by a tax collector to protect him while he worked. Now you know why they call them Doberman Pinchers- anybody the tax guy visited felt the pinch.

Trivia Treats

German inventor Stephan Lict was granted a patent for a "harness for dog-wearing sunglasses" in 2003.

The Germans were the first to use guide dogs, trained to assist blind war veterans following World War I.

Snoopy first made his appearance in Charles Schulz' *Peanuts* on October 4, 1950. Schulz planned to call him "Sniffy" until he discovered that name in a different comic strip.

celebrating DOGS

I have found that when you are deeply troubled, there are things you get from the silent devoted companionship of a dog that you can get from no other source.

-Doris Day

Tales of Tails

Labradors, Pointers, Setters, Foxhounds and Beagles are prone to a temporary condition known as "frozen tail." This results when the overused muscles of the tail cause it to hang limply.

When two dogs meet, the one wagging its tail very slowly is apt to be the dominant one.

A dog's tail is a means of communication but a Retriever gets some extra use of it as a rudder when in the water.

A dog says more with his tail in moments than his master can say with his tongue in hours. *–Rory Tomlinson*

The reason a dog has so many friends is that he wags his tail instead of his tongue. *–Unknown*

Dogs laugh, but they laugh with their tails. *–Max Eastman*

A fellow wanted the vet to cut his dog's tail off. The vet asked why. He said, "Well, my mother-in-law is visiting next month and I want to eliminate any possible indication that she is welcome."

celebrating DOGS

Dog lovers are a good breed themselves.
-Gladys Taber

While swimming comes naturally for most dogs, heavier breeds such as Bassets and French Bulldogs are more likely to sink than to float.

All breeds of dog have been found to attack livestock - from 3 - month- old puppies, all the way up to thirteen -year -old poodles.

Smaller breeds mature faster than larger breeds.

Boxers are so named because of their manner of playing with their front paws.

The Basenji is known as the African Barkless dog because it yodels instead of barking.

Technically all dogs, from the St. Bernard to the Chihuahua, belong to the same species. They all descended from wolves and can thus interbreed.

celebrating **DOGS**

While small breeds are gaining in popularity, the big breeds are still top dog with the most popular breeds in order being: 1. the Labrador Retriever 2.Golden Retriever and 3. German Shepherd.

Labrador Retrievers were originally bred to retrieve fishing nets.

The Great Dane is a German breed, not Danish, and the Australian Shepherd is American.

The rare Japanese Tosa was initially bred for dog wrestling, an ancient tradition used to inspire Samurai warriors. Dogs took part in formal matches, wore ceremonial robes, and could be disqualified for barking or growling.

Pharaoh Hounds have a very rare trait of "blushing", as their ears and nose become bright pink when they are excited or happy.

The Irish Wolfhound is considered the world's tallest dog breed, with a shoulder height for males of 32 inches.

There are 701 types of pure breed dogs.

The "spring" in Springer Spaniel referred to the breed's ability to spring or startle game.

celebrating DOGS

The pug is living proof that God has a sense of humor.
–*Margot Kaufman*

I have a great dog. She's half Lab, half pit bull. A good combination. Sure, she might bite off my leg, but she'll bring it back to me.
–*Jimi Celeste*

My dog is half pit bull, half poodle. It's not much of a watchdog, but it's a vicious gossip. –*Craig Shoemaker*

I wonder if other dogs think poodles are members of a weird religious cult. –*Rita Rudner*

Trivia Treats

Female dogs are only "in heat"- that is, ready to mate - twice a year for a total of approximately 20 days.

Dogs judge objects first by their movement, then by their brightness, and lastly by their shape.

City life is the good life for dogs - at least in terms of longevity. Dogs live about three years longer in the city than in country areas.

Top 10 Reasons Dogs Are Better Than Cats

(In fact, they may be better than anything!)

#10. If you feed, love, lavish with toys and treats, play with and take care of a dog, he thinks you're a God. Do the same thing for a cat and he thinks he's a God.

#9. Dogs regard you as their owner and master; cats consider you but a servant and slave.

#8. Dogs might bring you the newspaper. Cats might bring you a dead mouse.

#7. Dogs sit on your lap for love. Cats sit there because it's the warmest spot in the house.

#6. When you have to give a cat a pill, you need a crowbar to pry

celebrating DOGS

open its jaws, a vise to hold its head still, a suit of armor to protect you from the claws and a small hydraulic ram to jam the pill down its throat. When you have to give a pill to a dog, simply wrap it in bacon.

#5. Dogs come when called. Cats just yawn and roll over.

#4. Dogs will allow you to give them a bath without taking out a contract on your life.

#3. Dogs welcome you home from a long hard day at work; cats pretend never to have noticed that you were even gone.

#2. Dogs will sit, heel and lie down on command. Cats will smugly walk away.

And the #1 Reason Dogs Are Better Than Cats...

Dogs will bark like crazy to wake you up if the house is on fire. Cats will ever so quietly sneak out the back door.

celebrating DOGS

Screen Test

Take Two

1. In which film would you find Pongo and Perdita?

2. Which film thoroughfare would you likely find Toto on?

3. Name the three-headed dog that guarded the Philosopher's Stone at Hogwarts in the Harry Potter films.

4. Remember the name of the older dog voiced by Don Ameche in *Homeward Bound*?

5. What kind of dog was Old Yeller?

ANSWERS:

1. *101 Dalmatians* 2. The Yellow Brick Road- it wasn't Toto's doing- it was the Wizard of Oz. 3. Fluffy 4. Shadow 5. Golden Retriever

celebrating DOGS

Love Is A Three-Letter Word

For me a house or an apartment becomes a home when you add one set of four legs, a happy tail, and that indescribable measure of love that we call a dog. *–Roger Caras*

Dogs are forever in the moment. They are always a tidal wave of feelings and every feeling is some variant of love. *–Cynthia Heimel*

The average dog has one request to all humankind. Love me. *–Helen Exler*

A dog is the only thing on earth that loves you more than you love yourself. *–Josh Billings*

A dog is like an eternal Peter Pan, a child who never grows old and who therefore is always available to love and be loved. *–Aaron Katcher*

celebrating DOGS

The greatest love is a mother's; then a dog's; then a sweet-heart's. *–Polish Proverb*

No one can really understand the meaning of love unless he's owned a dog. A dog can show you more honest affection with a flick of his tail than a man can gather through a lifetime of handshakes. *–Gene Hill*

Our dogs will love and admire the meanest of us, and feed our colossal vanity with their uncritical homage. *–Agnes Repplier*

Money will buy you a fine dog, but only love can make its tail wag. *–Richard Friedman*

Dogs love their friends and hate their enemies, quite unlike people, who are incapable of pure love and always have to mix love and hate. *–Sigmund Freud*

Unconditional love: When I think of those two words, I think of one word- dog. *–Jack Kreismer*

celebrating DOGS

POLITICALLY CORRECT

If you want to find a friend in Washington, get a dog.
–*Harry Truman*

What counts is not necessarily the size of the dog in the fight - it's the size of the fight in the dog. –*Dwight D. Eisenhower*

Any man who does not like dogs and want them about does not deserve to be in the White House. –*Calvin Coolidge*

I love a dog. He does nothing for political reasons. –*Will Rogers*

Children and dogs are as necessary to the welfare of the country as Wall Street and the railroads. –*Harry S Truman*

My advice to any diplomat who wants to have good press is to have two or three kids and a dog. –*Carl Rowan*

celebrating DOGS

For the Record

The world's smallest dog, in length, is Heaven Sent Brandy, a female Chihuahua owned by Paulette Keller, which measured 6 inches from the nose to the tip of her tail on January 31, 2005.

In 2004, a Neopolitan mastiff named Tia gave birth to 24 puppies, the largest litter ever.

On July 6, 2003, a Golden Retriever from Dallas, Texas, by the name of Augie set the dog's world record for holding tennis balls in the mouth- 5.

Here's a record that is dog-eared, literally. Tigger the Bloodhound, owned by Bryan and Christina Flessner of St. Joseph, Illinois, measured in with the longest dog ears in the world- 13.75 inches and 13.5 inches for his right and left ears, respectively.

Star Title of Australia has been clocked at the fastest speed ever for a dog. The greyhound was timed at 41.38 miles per hour in Australia on March 5, 1994.

celebrating DOGS

In the records you never knew existed department: A Cocker Spaniel holds the world mark for the most persistent barking- 907 times in 10 minutes.

An Australian cattle-dog named Bluey, owned by Les Hall of Rochester, Victoria, Australia, was obtained as a puppy in 1910 and worked among cattle and sheep for nearly 20 years. He was put to sleep on November 14, 1939 at the age of 29 years, 5 months, the oldest dog ever.

Trivia Treats

The Chihuahua is the only natural toy breed- in other words, the only toy breed that wasn't bred down to its small size.

The Girl Scouts and Boy Scouts both offer merit badges in dog care.

The first seeing-eye dog was given to a blind person on April 25, 1938.

At Key Underwood Coon Dog Memorial Graveyard in Alabama, only a single breed of dog, Coonhounds, are allowed to be buried.

celebrating DOGS

If you can resist treating a rich friend better than a poor friend,

If you can face the world without lies and deceit,

If you can say honestly that deep in your heart you have no prejudice against creed, color, religion or politics,

Then, my friend, you are almost as good as your dog.

—Unknown

celebrating **DOGS**

You Da' Man

You can say any foolish thing to a dog, and the dog will give you this look that says, 'My God, you're right! I never would've thought of that!' *–Dave Barry*

No one appreciates the very special genius of your conversation as a dog does. *–Christopher Morley*

The dog is a yes-animal, very popular with people who can't afford to keep a yes-man. *–Robertson Davies*

Dog is the only animal in the world who ostensibly likes another breed better than his own. Man. *–Ted Patrick*

Let's examine the dog mind: Every time you come home, he thinks it's amazing. He can't believe that you've accomplished this again. You walk in the door. The joy of it almost kills him. 'He's back again! It's that guy! It's that guy!' *–Jerry Seinfeld*

celebrating **DOGS**

FOOD FOR THOUGHT

My dog is worried about the economy because Alpo is up to $3.00 a can. That's almost $21.00 in dog money. *–Joe Weinstein*

Most vegetarians frown upon a vegetarian diet for dogs, as they're natural carnivores and may develop intestinal gas problems if on a meatless regimen.

The Polish lowland sheepdog in present day Poland has a prescribed diet consisting of bread, potatoes, milk, cottage cheese and an occasional egg.

Chocolate, grapes and raisins can all be poisonous to dogs if ingested in large quantities.

Don't add onion rings to Fido's food list. The high levels of sulfur compound can damage a dog's red blood cells and cause hemolytic anemia.

celebrating DOGS

The Parts Of Its Sum

Dogs have three eyelids. They have an upper and lower eyelid and a third one inside of the other two for extra protection from dirt and dust.

Dogs have twice as many muscles for moving their ears as humans.

Nose prints are the best way to identify dogs as they are as unique to dogs as fingerprints are to humans.

Inbreeding causes 30% of Dalmatian dogs to suffer from hearing loss.

Dogs are not, in fact, colorblind. They don't see reds and greens, much as we don't at twilight.

Researchers have shown that dogs, using their swiveling ears, can locate the source of a sound in 6/100ths of a second. That's how they can be at the electric can opener before you even realize it's running.

A dog's whiskers are called vibrissae, touch-sensitive hairs that can actually recognize tiny changes in airflow.

Even though they sometimes have very large tongues, dogs have relatively few taste buds ... about 1,700 to our 9,000.

A dog's sense of hearing is over ten times more acute than a human's.

Temperature and diet can affect the pigmentation of a dog's nose, causing it to fade temporarily or even permanently.

A "dewlap" is the pendulous fold of skin on the neck, like you would see on a Bloodhound.

Canines with the best eyesight? Greyhounds rule.

celebrating DOGS

SIMPLY PUT

Dogs are miracles with paws. *–Susan Ariel Rainbow Kennedy*

Scratch a dog, and you'll find a permanent job. *–Franklin P. Jones*

A man's soul can be judged by the way he treats his dog.
–Charles Doran

The most affectionate creature in the world is a wet dog.
–Ambrose Bierce

My idea of good poetry is any dog doing anything. *–J. Allen Boone*

The fidelity of a dog is a precious gift. *–Konrad Lorenz*

Only my dogs will not betray me. *–Maria Callas*

A house is not a home until it has a dog. *–Gerald Durrell*

Dogs are not our whole life, but they make our lives whole.
–Roger Caras

celebrating DOGS

A Titanic Hero

Rigel, a Newfoundland owned by the first officer of the Titanic, Lieutenant William Murdock, reportedly saved many lives after the ship had sunk. Rigel was in the water for quite a spell, looking for his master who had gone down with the ship. In the night, the rescue ship Carpathia nearly ran into one of the lifeboats but crewmen heard Rigel barking, thus alerting them of the possible collision and saving numerous passengers.

Unleashed Thoughts

They have dog food for constipated dogs. If your dog is constipated, why screw up a good thing? Stay indoors and let 'em bloat!
–David Letterman

There are 206 bones in the adult human body. If you want an interesting experience sometime, just tell your dog that. *–George Gobel*

I spilled spot remover on my dog. He's gone now. *–Steven Wright*

Dogs need to sniff the ground; it's how they keep abreast of current events. The ground is a giant dog newspaper, containing all kinds of late breaking dog news items, which, if they are especially urgent, are often continued in the next yard. *–Dave Barry*

Did you ever walk into a room and forget why you walked in? I think that is how dogs spend their lives. *–Sue Murphy*

I like driving around with my two dogs, especially on the freeways. I make them wear little hats so I can use the carpool lanes. *–Monica Piper*

celebrating DOGS

I just bought a Chihuahua. It's the dog for lazy people. You don't have to walk it. Just hold it out the window and squeeze.
–Anthony Clark

If dogs could talk, it would take a lot of the fun out of owning one.
–Andy Rooney

Did you ever notice when you blow in a dog's face he gets mad at you? But when you take him in a car he sticks his head out the window. –Steve Bluestein

Dog is God spelled backwards. That means something, I'm just not sure what exactly, but human is namuh spelled backwards.
–Marc-Christophe Wagner

I went to an exclusive kennel club. It was very exclusive. There was a sign out front: "No Dogs Allowed." –Phil Foster

I bought my grandmother a Seeing Eye dog. But he's a little sadistic. He does impressions of cars screeching to a halt. –Larry Amoros

I looked up my family tree and found three dogs using it.
–Rodney Dangerfield

celebrating DOGS

Double Feature

In the midst of World War I, in 1918, Corporal Lee Duncan and his battalion visited a bombed war dog kennel in Lorraine, France. The only living animals they found were a German shepherd dog named Betty and her litter of five ten-day-old puppies. While the entire family was rescued, only one of the puppies would survive. The lucky dog's name…Rin Tin Tin. Credited with saving Warner Brothers from bankruptcy, the pooch would make twenty-six pictures for the studio, earning an astounding $2,300 a week at the peak of his career. After his death, his descendents, including Rin Tin Tin Jr. and Rin Tin Tin IV, would go on to entertain audiences for decades to come.

The character of Lassie was created by British-American author Eric Knight in "Lassie Come Home", a short story published in the *Saturday Evening Post* in 1938 and then made into a bestselling novel in 1940. The film rights to Knight's story of a young Yorkshire boy and his loyal collie would be purchased for $10,000 by MGM. The first dog to play the 1943 movie role of Lassie was "Pal". Nine direct descendants of Pal performed as Lassie, and all nine were male, playing a female character. Possible explanations for this include the male's larger size, as a child actor could play opposite the dog for a longer period of time. In addition, the female collie loses her coat at least once a year, making it unsuitable for use year round.

Trivia Treats

Lassie was the first animal named to the Animal Hall of Fame in 1969.

Cartoon canines: Dennis the Menace's dog is named Gnasher and Dagwood Bumstead's is Daisy

Walt Disney's family poodle was named Lady.

celebrating **DOGS**

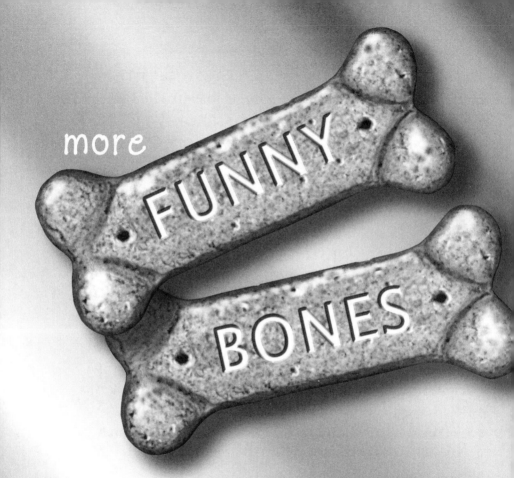

more FUNNY BONES

Then there was the insomniac who was an agnostic dyslexic. He stayed up all night wondering about the meaning of Dog.

The former Taco Bell Chihuahua, a German shepherd, and a Bulldog are hanging out at a doggie bar, lapping back a few cool ones when a good-looking female French Poodle comes up to them and says, "Whoever can say 'liver' and "cheese' in a sentence can take me back to his dog house."
So the German shepherd says, "I love liver and cheese."
The Poodle says, "Sorry, that's not good enough."
The Bulldog says," I hate liver and cheese."
She says, "That's not good enough either."
Finally the Chihuahua says, "Liver alone...cheese mine! "

A man takes his Dachshund to the vet and says, "My dog is cross-eyed. Is there anything you can do for him?"
The vet says, "Well, let's have a look."
The vet picks the dog up and examines his eyes. Finally he says "I'm going to have to put him down."
"What?" the man protested in horror. "Just because he's cross-eyed?"
"No," replied the vet," because he's really, really heavy."

celebrating DOGS

Then there was the girl who named her dog Seiko. Of course, it was a watchdog.

How come the cowboy bought a dachshund?
Someone told him to get a long little doggy.

An eighty-year-old woman sat in her rocking chair quietly passing the evening with her dog in front of the fireplace.
Suddenly, her Fairy Godmother appeared. "I can grant any three wishes you desire," said the Fairy Godmother. "Choose carefully."
The old woman thought for a moment and said, "Well, I'd like to be rich."
Poof! All the furniture in her home turned into solid gold.
"And I guess I'd like to be young again."
Poof! She was immediately twenty years old again.
"And, I guess now that I'm young and rich, I'd really like a lover."
Poof! Her dog changed into a drop-dead, gorgeous prince. She suddenly was mad with desire. The prince glided over to the woman, brushed his lips against her ear seductively and whispered, "Now aren't you sorry you had me neutered?"

celebrating **DOGS**

A traveling salesman came up to an old man rocking on his front porch but stopped short when he spotted a rather large and fierce looking dog.

"Excuse me, sir," the salesman called out. "Does your dog bite?"

"Nope," the old man answered.

The salesman straightened his phony grin and confidently strode up the steps. With that, the dog jumped at him and buried his teeth in the salesman's backside.

"Hey, I thought you said your dog didn't bite," complained the salesman.

The old man looked up and said, "It ain't my dog."

Did you hear about the dog that requires three baths a day? It's called a Shampoodle.

Two hillbillies were having a conversation. The first hillbilly says, "You know, it's a dog-eat-dog world out there."

The second one says, "Yeah, but it could be worse. It could be the other way around."

What do you call religious leaders in Munich?
German Shepherds

THE FAMOUS AND THEIR FRIENDS

Owner	Dog's Name	Breed
Jessica Alba	Sid	Pug
Jennifer Aniston	Norman	Corgi-Terrier mix
Jimmy Buffet	Cheeseburger	Golden Retriever
Jim Carrey	George	Great Dane
Mariah Carey	Jack	Jack Russell Terrier
Gloria Estafan	Noelle	Bulldog
Brett Favre	Jazzmin	Yorkshire Terrier
Michael J. Fox	Bosco	Dalmatian
Jennifer Garner	Martha Stewart	Labrador
Wayne Gretzky	Clyde	Dachshund
Ken Griffey, Jr.	Akeiba	Rottweiler
Janet Jackson	Buckwheat, Puffy	Chow Chow, Mixed Breed

celebrating DOGS

Owner	Dog's Name	Breed
Ashley Judd	Buttermilk	Cock-a-Poo
Matt Lauer	Walden	Golden Retriever
Lindsay Lohan	Chloe	Maltese
Nicole Richie	Honeychild	Shih tzu
Joan Rivers	Spike	Yorkshire Terrier
Pete Sampras	Samantha	Yellow Labrador Retriever
Adam Sandler	Matzoball	Bulldog
Ashlee Simpson	Blondie	Maltipoo
Jessica Simpson	Daisy	Maltipoo
Will Smith	Indo and Zhaki	Rottweilers
Britney Spears	Bit Bit	Chihuahua
Oprah Winfrey	Sophie, Solomon	American Cocker Spaniels
Reese Witherspoon	Frank Sinatra	English Bulldog

celebrating DOGS

Party Animal

It is fatal to let any dog know that he is funny, for he immediately loses his head and starts hamming it up.
–P.G. Wodehouse

Dogs love company. They place it first on their short list of needs. *–J.R. Ackerley*

It's impossible to keep a straight face in the presence of one or more puppies. *–Unknown*

Thomas A. Edison was once reluctantly persuaded by his wife to attend one of the big social functions of the season in New York. At last the inventor managed to escape the crowd of people vying for his attention, and sat alone unnoticed in a corner. Edison kept looking at his watch with a resigned expression on his face. A friend edged near to him unnoticed and heard the inventor mutter to himself with a sigh, "If there were only a dog here!" *–Edmund Fuller*

celebrating DOGS

WHO TRAINS WHO?

A woman once returned a book in extremely tattered condition to the Stroud Library in Gloucestershire, England. She blamed it on the dog, explaining that it had chewed on the manual. The book's title: *How to Train Your Dog.*

In dog training, jerk is a noun, not a verb. *–Dr. Dennis Fetko*

A well-trained dog will make no attempt to share your lunch. He will just make you feel so guilty that you will not enjoy it. *–Helen Thomson*

I have a dog, and I've trained him to go on paper, but he won't wait until I've finished reading it. *–Richard Jeni*

A dog teaches a boy fidelity, perseverance, and to turn around three times before lying down. *–Robert Benchley*

In order to really enjoy a dog, one doesn't merely try to train

celebrating DOGS

him to be semi human. The point of it is to open oneself to the possibility of becoming partly a dog. –*Edward Hoagland*

We have a huge family dog. He doesn't allow us to sit on the sofa. –*Eric Lehmann*

Canine Cunning

Men cannot think like dogs... (there is) a sharp difference in the mental capacity of humans and canines. For example, a human who is given an intricate problem will spend all day trying to solve it, but a canine will have the sense to give up and do something else instead. –*Cory Ford*

A Canadian psychologist is selling a video that teaches you how to test your dog's IQ. Here's how it works: If you spend $12.99 for the video, your dog is smarter than you. –*Jay Leno*

If you think dogs can't count, try putting three dog biscuits in your pocket and then giving Fido only two of them. –*Phil Pastoret*

celebrating DOGS

It is my experience that in some areas [my poodle] Charley is more intelligent that I am, but in others he is abysmally ignorant. He can't read, can't drive a car, and has no grasp of mathematics. But in his own field of endeavor, which he is now practicing, the slow, imperial smelling over and anointing on an area, he has no peer. Of course his horizons are limited, but how wide are mine?
–*John Steinbeck*

I myself have known some profoundly thoughtful dogs.
–*James Thurber*

Stanley Coren's book *Why We Love the Dogs We Do* says the average dog understands about 200 words and has the intelligence level of a 2-year old child.

An Animal Hospital Association survey reveals that dogs generally score higher on IQ tests than cats.

While canines may top felines in many intelligence areas, University of Michigan tests concluded that cats have better memories than dogs. A dog's memory lasts no more than five minutes while a cat's can last as long as 16 hours!

celebrating **DOGS**

In order, the world's smartest dogs are thought to be: the Border Collie, the Poodle, and the Golden Retriever. Meanwhile, the dog believed to be the most mentally challenged is the Afghan hound.

Trivia Treats

U.S. patent number 5,023,850 was granted to Rodney H. Metts and Barry D. Thomas on June 11, 1991, for their invention of a Dog Watch, described as "A novelty clock, watch, and the like for keeping time at an animal's rate, defined in terms of a multiple of human rate by dividing the average lifetime of a particular animal into the average lifetime of a human being." Translated, the watchdog, er dogwatch, multiplies by seven, because humans, as the theory goes, live seven times as long as dogs. A drawing accompanying the patent document shows "a wristwatch worn by a typical dog."

Portuguese Water Dogs are used to retrieve baseballs hit out of the park and into the water known as McCovey Cove, at AT&T Park, home of the San Francisco Giants.

celebrating DOGS